Contents

D1809891

Our Cover Pictures: Front—Clipping at Dry Howe, Selside (J. Hardman). Back—Horned Cattle at Netherwasdale (Ivor Nicholas).

FREE-RANGE HENS AT ROSTHWAITE, BORROWDALE

Introduction and Acknowledgements

SINCE the magazine *Cumbria* was established some 30 years ago, thousands of photographs have been submitted for use, and a remarkably high number of them pictured the people of the Lake District at work and play. It is from this group – this evocation of the traditional way of life – that my selection has been made. The prints recall Lakeland customs which, though historically recent, now charm us by their quaintness. Rapid changes in the Lake District have left many of our older folk feeling bemused and somewhat isolated.

I have concentrated on the native folk: on those who lived in Lakeland by the right of many generations. The activities shown are of a traditional kind, unaltered in their basic form over a considerable span of years. Through these pictures, we have an authentic review of the fundamental aspects of Lakeland life, those which distinguished the region from other parts of the North Country. It was for much of the time a courageous response to the bleak and impoverished state of the land and a fickle climate.

Modern visitors to Lakeland can observe a continuation of this Lakeland way of life at the rural shows, the sports, the open days at our farms, and the several notable museums and galleries. On our fell farms, men and their dogs still tend the Herdwick sheep in the time-honoured way, on foot, and no one has yet devised a machine for repairing a gap in a drystone wall.

Gone are some of the old crafts and industries, and yet much of the old folk life remains. The wrestlers still demonstrate their ancient skills at Grasmere, the rush-bearers process in several Lakeland towns and villages, trail hounds follow a delicate scent laid across the hills and are greeted rapturously by their owners as they return to the showfield.

The native folk cling stubbornly to their heritage. For many, *their* Lakeland was that before the creation of the county of Cumbria, when the district was divided between Cumberland, Westmorland and Lancashire. They remember when every parish had a lusty life of its own. Throughout its existence, the magazine *Cumbria* has been concerned to portray the native folk and their lives. Most of the pictures in this collection are of quite ordinary people in their everyday activity.

I must thank the many photographers whose work appears in this book. Their names and contributions are listed here:

A. Morrell, 26; G. Bertelsman, 27, 41 (right); The National Trust, 30; Russell Horton, 32 (left); Cyril Harrington, 36 (bottom left), 63; Geoffrey N. Wright, 38 (right), 57 (right); Christopher Stringer, 42 (bottom right), 69; F. S. Hardman, 48 (top right); Gordon Wood, 48 (bottom); Colin Denwood, 49 (right), 59 (left), 71 (top left), 77 (top left), 78 (left).

E. M. Monsarrat, 1, 73 (top right); Harold D. Bowtell, 50 (top); S. H. Cole, 2, 49 (left), 67 (left); Glenn B. Clarkson, 52 (top left); J. Penny, 3, 59 (right); Derek Cross, 53; John P. Delaney, 4, 22 (bottom), 46, 47; J. A. Tweats, 57 (bottom left); Ivor Nicholas, 6, 8, 45, 54 (left), 64 (right), 78 (top); W. R. Mitchell, 7 (left), 16 (top left), 18 (top right), 21, 28, 31, 32 (right), 33, 37, 37 (left), 42 (bottom left), 43 (left), 44, 54 (right), 55 (top), 64 (left), 65, 75, 76; T. Parker, 7 (right), 9 (left), 23 (right), 25, 29, 36 (top left), 36 (right), 40, 41 (left), 48 (top left), 52 (bottom), 56 (top), 62 (bottom), 70, 71 (bottom left), 73 (bottom right), 77 (bottom left), 77 (right).

Derek Widdicombe, 9 (right); Noel Habgood, 79; J. H. Cookson, 10, 12 (bottom); A. Stephens, 12 (top left), 68 (top); P. Walshaw, 80; Abraham Collection, 13 (left); J. Crowe, 13 (bottom right); Richard Clapham, 58; Sankey Collection, 14, 51; F. H. Marchbank, 73 (left); G. H. Deason, 15; L. Hewkin, 16 (top right), 24, 55 (bottom); V. Lakey, 78 (bottom right); Windermere Steamboat Museum, 16 (bottom left); Cumbrian Tourist Board, 66 (left); Eric Kingsdale, 16 (bottom right), 34, 39 (right); Herbert Collection, 17 (top); R. D. Humber, 18 (left), 67 (right); Abbot Hall Gallery, 18 (bottom right); J. Hardman, 19, 35, 60, 71 (right); Lilian D. Douglas, 20; Sanderson and Dixon, 22 (top), 57 (top left), 74; W. S. Garth, 23 (left); L. R. Lane, 56 (bottom).

Lakeland Folk
at Home . . .

THE LAKELAND farmstead appeals to us because of its situation – often on a knoll, with a sycamore standing nearby, and the fellside rising not far from the back door – and because it demonstrates the unpretentious use of local materials – stone, slate and wood. The slate roof is well pitched to discourage snow to linger and to speed away the quite heavy rainfall; the walls are thick and, invariably, whitened. There is a slated porch to cheat the wind and to enable the farmer to sit down and remove his dirty boots and outer garments before entering the house.

Nearly every farm has metal hooks driven into the beams of the kitchen so that rolls and sides of pork can be suspended for a while after being salted. Pictured on the left are Mr. and Mrs. Tom Mason, of Seaton Hall, Bootle, with a valuable addition to the family's store of food.

Furnishings in a farmhouse were generally robust and simple, also reflecting the interest of the farmer in fox-hunting. This Patterdale farmer had collected a sporting print, the mask of a fox and a hunting horn. He is clearly a sheep farmer, proud of the shepherds' crooks he has made laboriously on dark winter evenings. Three of them are straight-forward crooks, useful to him when tending his flock on the fell, but the two propped against the wall are so well decorated they are clearly "setting off" crooks, or those made for competition at a summer show.

The farm pictured on the far right is Blea Tarn House, between Great and Little Langdale. A number of old farms have rounded rather than squared-up chimneys.

The farmer in the picture is setting off for a spell of shepherding while a youngster settles down to play. Life at remote and solitary farms calls for attitudes that are developed through a dale upbringing. Children at such farms used to walk several miles to school, except during a severe winter when the farm might be cut off for several days by drifts of snow.

THE KNOWLES FAMILY OF LOW KINMONT, CORNEY

Left: Two farmers in the Lyth Valley apply themselves to what used to be a prolonged task – preparing a sufficiently large stock of wood for the fire. Notice one farmer's boots and leather gaiters. Our picture was taken in spring, for the damson trees are a mass of white blossom.

Above: Over 300 years ago, Lady Anne Clifford had almshouses built at Appleby, providing homes for elderly ladies, one of whom is seen in the tiny chapel of the almshouse group.

THE TOLL BAR, LYTH, WITH FARMERS RETURNING
FROM KENDAL MARKET

Out and About

NOW THAT the car provides us with high mobility, it is difficult to imagine how isolated were many communities and farmsteads in the Lake District when the horse was master of the dusty road. Consider the photograph on the left, which features the only remaining toll house then in use in the county of Westmorland. The narrow road is covered with loose stone. The farmers in the traps are in their better clothes, but the gate-keeper – disturbed in her daily round – has emerged wearing print pinafore and with slippers on her feet. When the picture was taken, the charge for a car was 1s, for a motor cycle 3d, horse and cart 3d, cow 1d and sheep ½d.

A considerable variety of vehicles served as buses. The Porter service (top right) served the secluded valley of the Esk. Notice the can of petrol strapped to one of the running boards (supplies of petrol were once delivered to parts of Lakeland by horse and cart), and the folded canopy. This could be speedily raised if the weather became inclement. Early travellers remember the summer cloud of dust as vehicles used the unmetalled roads.

The bus service between Ambleside and Hawkshead was one of a great many established after the 1914-18 war. Some of them were run by ex-Servicemen. Regulations were few, and often several companies were in lively competition on the same route. The bus driver was not averse to waiting for a regular passenger who was late, or accommodating on the bus a variety of goods. On market day, farmers' wives entered the local bus carrying baskets of butter and eggs for sale.

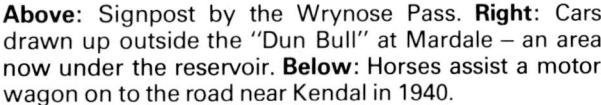

Above: Signpost by the Wrynose Pass. **Right**: Cars drawn up outside the "Dun Bull" at Mardale – an area now under the reservoir. **Below**: Horses assist a motor wagon on to the road near Kendal in 1940.

Above: Horse-drawn carriages on Honister Pass, between Borrowdale and Buttermere. **Above, right**: Transporting the body of huntsman Tommy Dobson over Hardknott (he died in Langdale). **Right**: Hardknott with its 1935-45 road surface.

A Day on the Lake

THE COMING of the railway to Windermere gave central Lakeland its mass appeal to holidaymakers. A host of people made directly for the lake, here to hire rowing boats or be taken for cruises on England's largest stretch of water.

Well-to-do folk who had bought land and built mansions were anxious to enjoy life on the lake in summer without having to forego some of the pleasures of the land or mix with the crowds arriving from Lancashire or West Yorkshire. The answer was to be found in having a private steamboat. Among the elegant craft that took to the water was *Britannia,* owned by the Ridehalgh family of Fell Foot. They were wealthy enough to maintain a big boat and also, periodically, to hire a band for the entertainment of their guests during a lake cruise.

There had been steamboats on Windermere since the first half of the 19th century. The present craft which runs a regular service on the lake date back to the period when the Furness Railway laid tracks to a terminus near the outflow of Windermere; it became known as Lakeside. Two of the craft in use today are of Furness Railway origin, the other two (larger) boats dating to the 1930s.

No longer does the crew of such a boat have to spend the end of the working day transporting coal from the shore to the bunkers, for all the craft have been fitted with diesel engines. No longer do passengers have to clean themselves down, as they did when a funnel suddenly emitted a cloud of soot!

There were characters among members of the steamboat crews. One, who noticed a passenger looking fixedly over the side, asked him the reason for his curiosity about the lake and was told that he had just lost a valuable watch over the side. The sailor said that if he was given half a crown he would recover the watch when the lake was cleaned out at the end of the season. The passenger snorted and remarked that the lake was never cleaned out. The sailor, pointing to the hills, said: "That's where we put the muck!"

Steamboats were launched on other lakes. The Furness Railway had the "Gondola" built for Coniston Water, and this craft has been restored for lake service by The National Trust. Its most famous skipper was Captain Hammill. He served on the "Gondola" for some 50 years – without an accident.

Above, left: The old "Tern". **Right:** Another view of the "Tern". **Left:** The "Swift", which was built in 1900. **Below:** Captain Hammill with a model of the "Gondola", the iron-hulled craft built for service on Coniston Water.

Above, left: The ferryboat "Drake", which operates from a point just south of Bowness Bay to a landing beside the Ferry House, on the western shore. **Above, right**: Three regular ferrymen – J. Sharpe, J. Hartley, J. Bowman – on the last ferry crossing before the "Drake" was brought into service. **Below**: "The Esperance" on Windermere. She was built for Schneider, the Furness industrialist, who lived at Belsfield, overlooking Bowness Bay, and is preserved at the Windermere Steamboat Museum. **Right**: A Bank Holiday scene at the steamer pier at Glenridding, Ullswater, as the "Lady of the Lake" sails in to collect the last passengers of the day. Patterdale is in view beyond the water.

Above: In the winter of 1894-5, Windermere was thickly frozen from end to end, and a multitude of people took to the ice. That was also the winter when horse-drawn sleds were seen. This impressive turnout was photographed in what was normally Bowness Bay.

Right: The mass of vegetation on Derwentwater which was renowned as a "floating island". The visitor on our picture had planted a Union Jack there. Another "floating island", complete with a coverlet of birch trees, existed near the bottom end of Coniston Water, but it was washed ashore at Nibthwaite during a gale and "did not manage to free itself."

The char is a fish which inhabits the deeps and swims into shallower water only in the spawning season. In its normal haunts, it is caught by a Lakeland angler using a rod with a line of considerable length – a line held down by a lead weight and with shorter lines extending from it, to which are attached the bright spinners (above) and hooks. Below is a char pot of about 1880. Large quantities of "potted char" were once despatched from Lakeland to urban areas.

SKATING ON RYDAL WATER

PLOUGHING ON THE SHORES OF LOWESWATER

Horses at Work

THE PICTURE on the left shows two horses harnessed to a plough. On the lowland farms, horses of this size could be employed, but the animal most closely associated with Lakeland's hill areas is the fell pony (right), which is dark and stocky, growing to about 13.2 h.h. There was a time when each farmer kept two or three mares and bred from them.

Shepherds often rode ponies. The woman (pictured right) is seen leading a pony over the hill near her home, delivering hay to outlying stock. Fell ponies made good shaft animals, making them popular with urban traders, and colts were purchased by colliery owners and went down the pits. Half a century ago, there was little demand for fell ponies, and an animal "broken in to drive" was sold for about £40. Today, over a hundred ponies may be seen at the annual show of the Fell Pony Society, and prices are high.

A farm horse needed little "keep". For most of the year, it dined on grass or hay, but something more nourishing was provided before haytime or harvest, or when the horse was to be used for ploughing. Individual horses were well known to the local blacksmith, and in making a set of shoes he combatted faults in gait, and the consequences of injuries and disease. He might also be called upon to shoe animals not yet fully broken, and said (ruefully) that some farmers would go as far as getting a halter round a horse's head so that it could be led, struggling, to the smithy, where the blacksmith — in the course of putting on shoes – completed the breaking in process!

Each town had its horse fair, and for over 600 years Brough Hill Fair was the recognised market for the Dales cob and the wild, unbroken fell pony. Some breeders walked their stallions long distances, so that the farm mares could be served. If the stallion was a Shire, it might weigh about a ton.

Heavy horses were set to work ploughing, and a former farm labourer recalls setting out from the farmhouse at 8 a.m. and ploughing until noon. At 1 p.m., after dinner, the work resumed until 5-30 p.m. It was "a day's work to plough an acre. You couldn't do it with stiff ley, but ploughing came easier with stubble. My brother once ploughed six acres in five days, which was good going; it was warming up the horses as well as himself!"

Some Lakeland horses in action. **Opposite page**: Mr. William Thwaites seen ploughing near Grasmere, and a farmer at Grange-in-Borrowdale with a horse-drawn cart. **Left**: A mounted farmer and his dog follow a flock of ewes and lambs down the hill from Kirkstone Pass to Ambleside (Windermere is seen distantly). **Above**: A horse used for forestry work near Thirlmere.

FORKING THE BRACKEN HARVEST UNDER COVER

HAYMAKING SCENES IN THE WINSTER VALLEY

The one-horse machines were popular for many years on the hill farms; previously the work was performed by hand.

The Rushbearings

STREWING fresh rushes on the earthen floors of Cumbrian churches sweetened up the building and, though discontinued at most places, is still commemorated at Grasmere, Ambleside and in the Eden Valley.

In St. Mary's Church, Ambleside, can be seen a painting 26 feet long and about 12 feet high which uses the local Rushbearing as its theme. The mural was painted by Gordon Ransome, a student at the Royal College of Art, which had its headquarters in Ambleside during the 1939-45 war.

At Ambleside, the custom of Rushbearing at the old church, St. Anne's, continued after the church had been rebuilt and flagged in 1812. In 1835, the Rushbearing was stylised by the curate, Owen Lloyd, who composed a special hymn which is still used. Today, reeds and rushes gathered from the sides of lakes and tarns are woven with flowers on to wooden frames of various designs; these are referred to as "bearings". A procession begins near St. Mary's and tours the town. Then all the bearings are lifted high so that the assembled crowd can see them. The procession continues to the church, for a service, after which the bearings are left in church and all who have carried them receive gingerbread.

At Warcop, St. Peter's Day is celebrated with rush crosses and crowns of flowers. The bearing of rush crosses by small boys was introduced as recently as the 1930s, though the girls have been processing with their floral crowns for many more years. A procession ends at the church, where a Rush-bearing hymn is sung. Children move to the altar, presenting their crowns and crosses, which are stacked around the altar and later moved to be hung over the main doors to the church for almost a year until the bases of the crowns are required for another Rushbearing. The rushes scent the church for a few weeks until they become wizened.

At Rydal, the well-known Dora's Field was formerly known as The Rashfield; it was the place where rushes were gathered. One fascinating little theory insists that rushes were taken to our Cumbrian churches not for their sweetness but to provide warmth for the feet of the worshippers.

GRASMERE RUSHBEARING: BEARERS WITH A SHEET OF RUSHES

Rushbearing at Warcop, in the Eden Valley. Here the children process, the boys carrying crosses made of rushes, and the girls crowns of flowers.

Lakeland's Own Little Sheep

WALK ON THE craggy, central fells of Cumbria and it will not be long before you meet a Herdwick. This breed of sheep belongs to those fells by the right of well over 1,000 generations. Sometimes, the Herdwick will greet you with a decisive sneeze, as though disputing your right to be on its domain.

A primitive breed, with built-in hardiness, the Herdwick successfully performs a natural balancing act in areas where most breeds would quickly lose condition. It grazes up to around 3,000 feet above sea level. Over 200 inches of rain a year may fall on the hairy jacket that overlies a soft, creamy-white undercoat. The eyes of the Herdwick, which look as ancient as the rocks round about, are set in a frosty, grey-white face: a broad, kindly face, the appearance of which belies the incredible stamina of an animal that ranges the roof of England.

The Herdwick is parochial in the extreme, forming an intense love for the section of fell on which it was born, and where it drank in its mother's milk. So closely does it associate itself with the home plot that there might be an invisible fence around it. The heaf-going instinct has made it unnecessary for walls to be built between the fell-grazings. Herdwick farming is built on this instinct, to the extent that its continuity must be maintained. A certain number of sheep, of different ages, goes with the farm, to be accepted by the incoming owner or tenant, who in due course will hand over that precise number to his successor.

The Herdwick is not a rare breed, if you accept that the type of sheep in this category has less than 1,500 breeding ewes. The population of Herdwicks lies between 15,000 and 18,000, the majority of which now belong to the National Trust, through its ownership of 72 hill farms in Lakeland.

Beatrix Potter, from whom the Trust acquired a large estate in Herdwick country, was the first woman chairman of the Herdwick Sheep Breeders' Association, and a great populariser of the breed. When one of her show tups, "Wedgewood", died she actually sent an obituary to the *Westmorland Gazette.* In the Herdwick breed, only the tups (males) carry horns, which are smaller than those of other hill breeds. A tup in "show red" is an impressive creature, its stocky body standing four-square on thick, white legs. Such an animal tends to be individualistic, and can be a real "character".

VIEWING HERDWICKS ON A CHANGE OF FARM TENANCY

At the "Herdwick Royal". This is held in a roadside field near Boot, in Eskdale, and is mainly for the purpose of allowing farmers to hire tups for the coming mating season (the tups are returned to their rightful owners in spring). **Above:** The head of a fine tup. **Below:** Farmers discussing terms. **Right:** Grooming a tup before it is shown.

The Swill Makers

AMONG THE old woodland crafts of Furness, swill-making survived until quite recent times, and there are still men in the area who are capable of making this type of basket, which was popular in farming and horticulture.

Oak which had been growing for up to 20 years reached the swill-maker, who then split it into lengths and placed the strips in a long cast-iron boiler. The boiling process softened the wood. Then it was riven into strips for plaiting into the basket, the rim of which was formed of ash or hazel. To watch a craftsman at work was to marvel at a well-developed combination of eyes and hands. The swill-maker felt his way down a piece of timber to ensure that it was riven with the grain.

In the picture on the left, Miles Whinfield works on a swill. The other print on this page gives an indication of the equipment needed by the swill-maker, and also features a completed basket. The craftsman seen "riving" needs to feel his way along a piece of oak, or it would not peel away smoothly. Notice also how he has reinforced his legs with corduroy against the hardness of the wood. I know a Furness craftsman who is capable of making a swill using oak which has not been boiled; he "rives" the strips of oak without distortion, being continually aware of all the strains and stresses.

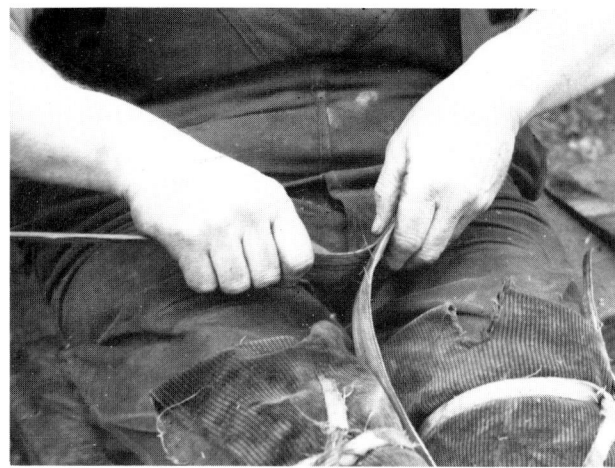

The old-time craftsmen were, in the main, a merry company of men. They worked calmly, smoothly in a rural setting, using native wood which came from the coppices and were clear-felled periodically to provide wood for a variety of uses, including the making of charcoal.

Lakeland Cattle

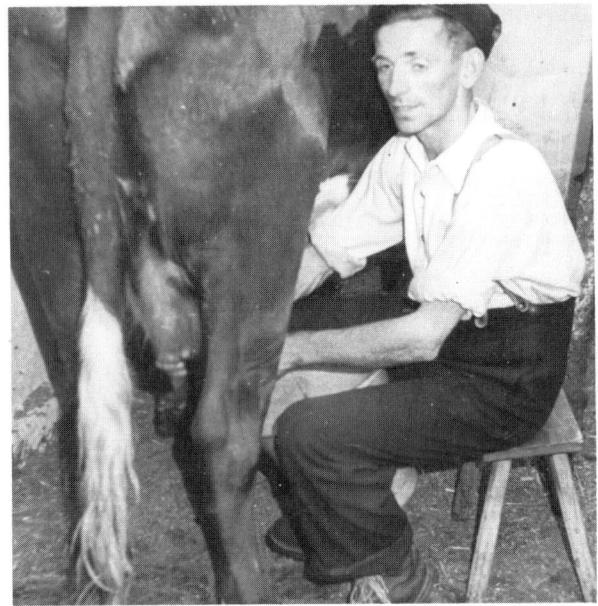

THE MAN seen hand-milking a cow in a Lakeland byre is Bill Teasdale, the fell-runner. Hand-milking of Shorthorn cattle ended recently enough for some not-so-old folk to recall it in detail. The photograph of cattle near Grasmere (right) is notable because those beasts are Shorthorns and retain their horns. The modern fashion is for dehorned Friesian cattle, which are milked by machine.

The Shorthorn was slowly evolved to suit the poorish land and often grim weather of the northern dales. It descended from stock improved by the 19th century breeders, and the first threat to the old type came in the 1930s, with the demand for more milk. A popular cross was with the Ayrshire, and the hybrid was successful in raising the average milk yield, but the characteristics of the Shorthorn breed were threatened; hence a meeting was held at Penrith in 1944 to form the Northern Dairy Shorthorn Breeders' Society.

The Shorthorn of the dales was both tough and thrifty. Its milk was rich in butterfat, being used to rear the calves and to make butter and cheese until the quite modern demand from the outside world for milk. In the slump early this century, good cows brought less than £20 each; prices soared in the 1914-18 war, but by the 1930s slump conditions had returned. Today, scarcely any Shorthorns remain.

Lakeland farmers remember when "beastings". the custard-like first flush of milk produced by a cow on calving, were made into an appetising pudding. Cream from the milk, separated by means of "leads", was made into dairy products sold in the nearest market town. It was often the grocer who took the butter and cheese, the value of which was set against the farmer's bill for provisions. Older folk remember when farmers' wives, with baskets of butter, cheese and eggs, "stood" the market.

Butter made at different farms could be readily identified by reference to a pattern imprinted upon each round pound. Butter prints, made of sycamore (a wood which does not taint milk), are now much prized collector's items.

SUMMER GRAZING NEAR RED BANK, GRASMERE

Above, left: White Shorthorns were not uncommon in Lakeland. **Left:** A herd of Shorthorns being driven up Boroughgate at Appleby. **Above:** A Borrowdale farmer and his son feeding the calves.

Stone and Slate

THE MORTARLESS WALLS of Lakeland lie in the upper dales like a futuristic pattern. They look to be half as old as time, and yet most of them date from the mid-18th to the mid-19th centuries. They were erected as boundaries, and yet they also provide shelter for stock at times when the weather is inclement.

A Lakeland wall is really two walls in one, built side by side, connected together by long stones known as "throughs", the centre filled with small pieces of stone and the wall capped off with large stones known as "cams", or coping stones. These are usually large stones stacked on edge, all leaning in the same direction. Notice also that apart from being pierced by gateways, some of our Lakeland walls have square holes left in the base. Known as hogg-holes (a hogg is a yearling sheep) they can be blocked when necessary by a large flat piece of stone but, when open, permit the farmer to graze both cattle and sheep, knowing that the cattle are restricted to one field but the sheep can, if necessary, wander through several fields.

It is interesting to speculate where the stones used in a stretch of wall were collected. First notice how the geology of the area is reflected in the type of material used. Then consider whether the stones are rounded or have edges. The rounded material almost certainly came out of the local beck. The squared material might have been quarried. A considerable amount of stone used in the early walls accumulated from the clearance of land for farming.

In some areas, notably Wasdale, much stone remained after the walls had been built, and so a small croft was formed of walls and the spare loose stones were piled within it. Jonathan Otley noted in 1818: "Wasdale Head comprises a level area of 400 acres of land divided by stone walls into irregular fields, which have been cleared with great industry and labour; as appears from the enormous heaps of stones, piled up from the surplus after completing the enclosure."

Slate-quarrying has for long been a major industry in Lakeland. It has, by and large, been a family occupation, with son following father in the craft. At places like Honister, visitors can watch men splitting slate into a thickness suitable for roofing purposes. Lakeland stone has in recent times been used for cladding the faces of large new buildings.

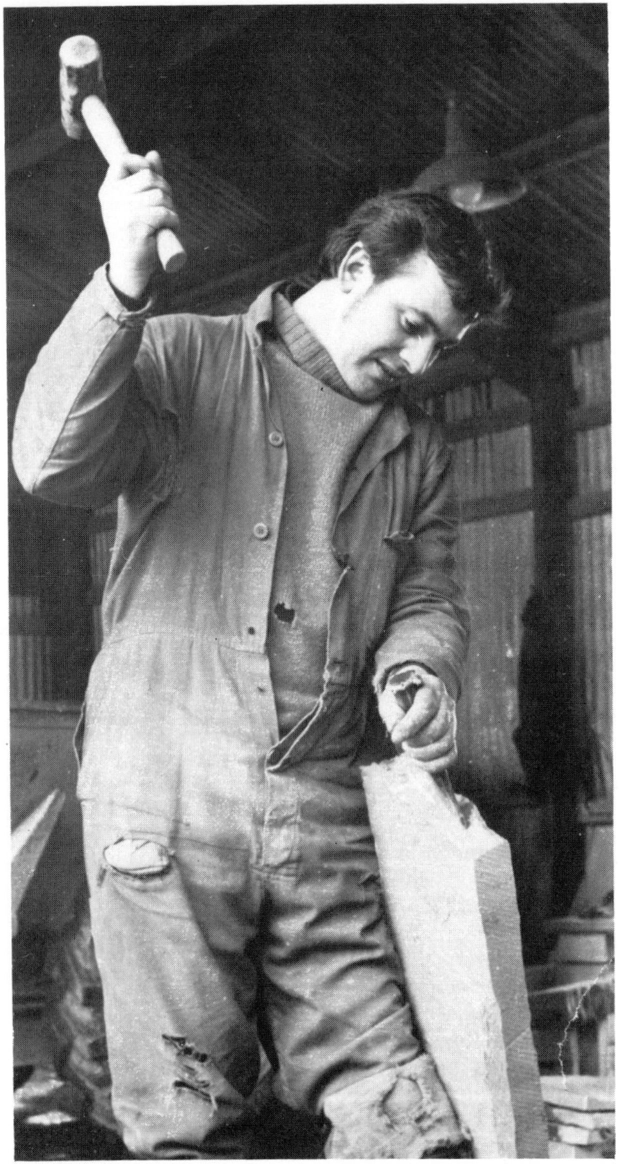

Left: Skill, not just brute strength, ensures success in the splitting, or "riving", of slate. This photograph was taken at a quarry near Elterwater. **Above**: Walkers in the Coniston area see much evidence of mining and quarrying. Here, on Coniston Old Man, we observe a ropeway from the mines. Also in view are the tracks of a narrow gauge railway on which moved the tubs.

Above: Slate from Honister Crag leaving the quarry for the splitting sheds, where it will be dressed. **Below**: A slate-dresser trimming the slate into its final shape. Notice the stack of slates waiting to be dressed (right) and the finished slates (left).

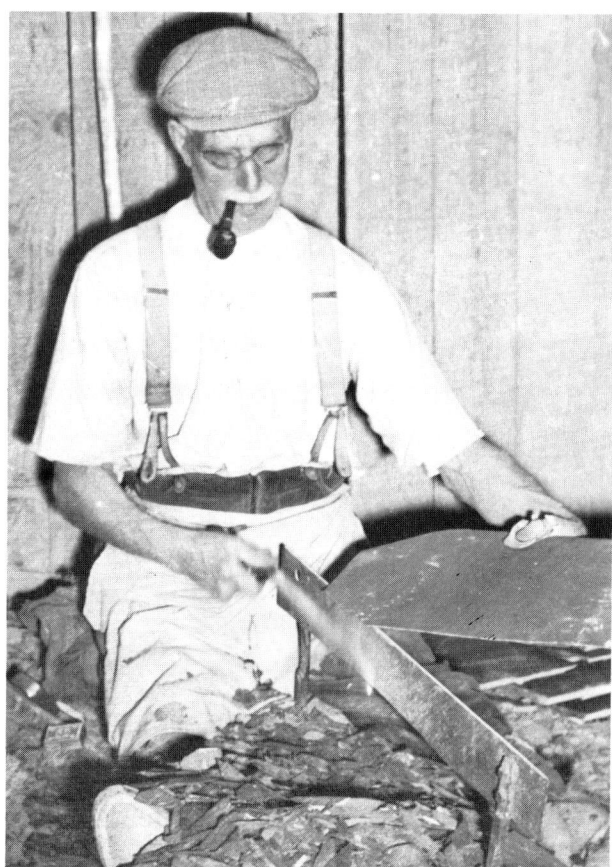

Above: Mr. Tom Cockbain Plaskett, of Rosthwaite, dressing slate at the Honister quarry. Lakeland slate has a delicate tonal range: olive-green at Broughton Moor, light green at Elterwater, green with markings at Spout Crag, black from Brathay, blue-grey from Kirkby, light green from Bursting Stone, olive-green from Moss Rigg, olive at Honister and light-green at Kirkstone.

The Flockmaster's Year

LAMBING TIME IN GREAT LANGDALE

Left: Anthony Barker, of Patterdale, with some of his Swaledale sheep. **Above**: A shepherd of old Cumberland. A Herdwick ewe carries its lamb for 20 of the grimmest weeks in the year. The nuptials are in November, or even December. No one expects the weather to improve until the birthtime in April, or even May, for spring is slow in coming to the fells and daleheads. A Herdwick lamb is a tiny black bundle of life whose immediate future depends on the speed with which its mother licks it dry and provides it with nourishing milk.

The Clipping

Once they clipped on stools, as in Little Langdale (right) and Newlands Vale (below). Later, clipping on the ground became usual (bottom right).

Clipping sheep near Buttermere (above) and in the
Duddon Valley (right).

On Show

Sheep prefer the open hill to a summer-time show. They soon become "show silly". Pictured on the right are some fine Herdwick tups at Boot, in Eskdale, while below some sheep of Swaledale type are being coaxed into a pen at the Rydal trials. The sheepdog, though not included in the picture, was undoubtedly inching itself forward behind the sheep.

HERDWICK TUPS AT KESWICK FAIR

At an autumnal tup-hiring, a bargain is made without recourse to documents and signatures. There may not even be a handclasp to seal it, but the few slowly uttered words are as binding as a farm tenancy. Neither farmer will think of violating the agreement.

Driving Sheep

GATHERING sheep from the open fells would be an almost impossible task were it not for the skill and stamina of the collie dog. The sheep (right) were being driven towards the old bridge at Watendlath. In a gathering, shrill whistles cut through the early morning air, which is often so calm that the sound carries for miles. The collies bark occasionally to rouse laggard or stubborn Herdwicks from the bracken patches and shadowy gills. An early morning start is important at gathering time. It will be a busy day, and if the work is delayed the sheep become languid in the full heat of the sun. Strays gathered up in autumn were once returned to their rightful owners at the Shepherds' Meets.

SHEEP ON THE OLD BRIDGE AT WATENDLATH

Left: Driving sheep in Longsleddale. **Above**: Sheep and lambs in Kentmere. **Below**: A round-up on the East Fellside.

Above: A sheep-salver, pictured in 1880. The salve – a mixture of grease and tar – was applied to the skin of a sheep, the wool having been parted, or "shedded", and a good salver could complete a single sheep in about an hour. The whole flock must be salved by tupping time.
Right: Sheep-dipping at Loweswater.

Between the Lines

THE MAIN LINES went over the Shap Fells, between Lancaster and Carlisle (London and North Western Railway) and up the Ribble and Eden Valleys in the east (Midland). The Furness Railway dominated the coastal region from Carnforth to Whitehaven, contrasting with the ramshackle collection of local lines which fought over the iron traffic of West Cumberland.

Visitors to Lakeland remember the delightful branch lines. One penetrated to Coniston, another terminated at Lakeside, and a third — reaching a point just east of Windermere — led to the rapid development of the area and the "borrowing" of the lake's title by the thrustful new community.

Pictured (left) is a "terminus in the fells": Coniston station, with its Swiss-chalet style of architecture and backcloth of mountains. This was perhaps the most attractive station in the Lake District. The line closed to passengers in 1958, and the station buildings have been demolished. Our photograph (bottom left) of Tebay, on the Lancaster-Carlisle line, shows a 2–6–4 tank engine about to bank a heavy goods train up the four miles of 1 in 75 to Shap summit. This stretch of the West Coast main line is now electrified.

The scene at Lakeside in about 1910 was photographed within a few yards of Windermere. It is now shorn of most of its original buildings, but still sees steam trains operated in the summer months by the Lakeside and Haverthwaite Railway. Ratty, a popular tourist attraction, extends (narrow gauge) from Ravenglass into Eskdale.

LAKESIDE STATION, ABOUT 1910

Above: One of the many attractively preserved loco-motives at Steamtown, Carnforth, a former engine shed which has become a live steam museum.

Above: At Tebay, a 4–6–0 locomotive prepares to work a coke train which has come over Stainmore summit from county Durham; it will take the train on to Barrow and Millom. **Below**: A "Jubilee" class locomotive heads a northbound express through the (then) tranquil surroundings of the Lune Gorge.

A TANK ENGINE WITH A WINDERMERE TO LONDON TRAIN.

Some Cumbrian Faces

Left: William Wilson was also known as Herdwick Billy because of his passionate interest in Lakeland's old sheep breed. There were even sheep in stained glass at his home near Bassenthwaite Lake. **Below:** A Patterdale farmer, his home tucked away in a side valley dominated by the high fells.

Above: Resident at a village on the East Fellside. **Above, right:** A retired farmer in Longsleddale, his head brushing the top of the door of his little, stone-built home. **Right:** The Harrison family of Brotherilkeld, upper Eskdale. Here are two parents and seven children, not forgetting the sheepdog.

A Time
for Harvest

IN THE stock-rearing areas of the upper dales, the vital crop is hay, and before the coming of machines the hay-making was a laborious hand operation. Pictured above are two farmers, raking hay into rows in a high meadow in Little Langdale, not far from Wrynose Pass. The single-horse mowing machine took much of the hard work out of haytime (grass was previously mown by hand), and our picture shows "Willie" Hawkrigg, of Bridge End Farm, St. John's Vale, turning at a corner.

Above: Loading a haycart at Low Wray Farm, near Ambleside.
Below: Making hay-pikes at a farm in the Eden Valley.
Right: Hay-pikes in the Newlands Valley on the evening of a good hay day.

Above, left: Building a stack at Strawberry Howe Farm, Cockermouth, about 1935. **Above**: A hand-driven threshing machine, found at a farm in the Whicham Valley, under Black Combe. Previously, the hand flail had been used.

Opposite page: Gathering bracken, to be used as bedding for the stock in winter. Our pictures show bracken at the stage of growth when it resembles a bishop's crozier; roping up heaps of bracken; and making the bracken stack at the farm. The bracken was cut, then left to dry, before being moved.

Outdoor Movement

Opposite page: Youth Hostellers at Winster. **Above, left**: T. A. Leonard, of the C.H.A., at Thorney How in 1932. **Above**: Kirkby Stephen Meeting House (a pioneer youth hostel occupied the top storey). **Below**: Lord Baden-Powell at the opening of Great Tower Plantation, above Windermere.

The Dog Months

THE DOG MONTHS are in late summer and early autumn – between the haymaking and the October sheep sales. It is the time when sheepdogs are on public view. Watch one of the events at a Lakeland sheepdog trial and you see the dogs that work by remote control. Go to a hound trail and see the hounds set off on a circuit which takes in the local hills; they follow a trail of aniseed laid down by men who have impregnated some sacking and drag it behind them as they lay out the course.

Our picture (above) shows Tommy Dobson and some hounds and terriers – also two supporters of the hunt – in Great Langdale. On the right is a print of men setting out for sheep gathering; they are shown as they trudge up Hardknott.

A well-trained sheepdog is almost beyond price. Few come on to the market. Some farmers train their own dogs, and have four or five in peak condition, but those who are too busy to devote time to this patient work will cheerfully pay a large sum for a well-broken animal that has the right temperament.

WITH DOG AND STICK AT A FARM NEAR GRASMERE

Scenes from a hound trail — the man with the "drag", hounds negotiating a fence, and the rapturous welcome home from the owners, who offer the hounds their favourite food.

Above: A rear view of Joe Wear, huntsman of the Ullswater, with attendant terriers. Such huntsmen were once so popular in a locality that ballads were composed about them, to be sung lustily whenever hunt supporters met at a Lakeland inn.

Above: The boot-encased feet of a dalesman who is about to follow a foxhunt. In Lakeland's dale country, this is hunting on foot. Also in the picture is a lively Lakeland terrier. The whipper-in at a hunt can cover many miles of difficult terrain. According to one huntsman, "he's t'chap 'at gits oot on t'tops!"

Food and Drink

MOST VISITORS will be familiar with the Cumberland sausage (above), which if properly made is "good enough to hod thi back up." The sign (pictured right) was seen outside one of Lakeland's best known hostelries, at Troutbeck.

Substantial fare was served to men working outdoors. Among the items cooked was the Cumberland hot-pot, into which went mutton, potatoes, carrots, onions, even black puddings. It looked unexciting at first, but then swelled and softened and browned, becoming a dish so firm that you could hardly sink a spoon into it!

Below: Some Lakeland folk, it should be whispered, distilled whisky without the knowledge of the law. Among them was a celebrated Lakelander called Lanty Slee, and this was a portable whisky-still he used. In earlier times, smuggling was an important trade, with spirits and other commodities being landed on quiet parts of the Cumbrian coast, to be borne inland on the backs of ponies. It was said that one consignment of whisky was temporarily stored in the local church.

Above: A metal cheese press, dating to the time in Lakeland when little milk left the farm as milk. Any that was spare was converted into butter or cheese. The weights suspended from one side of the press ensured that the cheese would be firmly pressed. Earlier presses had been made with stone as the weight.

The Festive Spirit

ENGLISH FOLK-DANCING has long been popular in central Lakeland, though not often nowadays does one see such a large crowd as was mustered at Grasmere in the Maytime of 1951. Garden parties have been well-supported in an area where there are many fine houses and gardens. Our group (right) was photographed when Myles Kennedy, of Stone Cross, Ulverston, threw open his garden for the benefit of local people about 1912.

Considerable skill, as well as strength, is needed by the wrestlers, Cumberland and Westmorland style, who delight the crowds at such events as Grasmere Sports, though the wrestlers pictured on the opposite page were performing at Rydal. Notice the traditional garb, and the fact that the wrestler on the left has his dark pants richly embroidered. It is said that this type of wrestling began when Jacob wrestled with the Angel!

WRESTLERS—CUMBERLAND AND WESTMORLAND STYLE—AT RYDAL

Travelling Folk

THEY ARE in the district — but not really of the district. The travelling folk appear when the old fairs are held at Appleby and Brough. Once the visitors had atttractive, horse-drawn vardo's, of the type pictured on the right. Now most of them arrive in modern caravans, drawn by motor vehicles.

The fair is a massive inconvenience for the good folk of Appleby, but the visitors enjoy what is truly a spectacle. Many hundreds of families are here, sitting around, gossiping about what has happened since last they met, or watching as the horse dealers trot their animals up and down before the critical gaze of potential buyers. Horses are run to confirm that they are sound and have a good action; they also attract attention, as a horse that is standing still never would. There is much haggling, and quite often the old-style handclasp seals a bargain.

Down in Appleby, horses are ridden into the Eden to be washed. The local shops and inns are crowded with travellers, who at this time are great spenders. Much of the surplus cash is locked up in such valuable objects as china cups and plates. The police maintain a good-natured vigil.

Brough Hill Fair, held in the autumn, is far less important than it was. At the edge of living memory, a huge crowd of dealers was here; it was predominently a business meeting rather than a social occasion. A person who went to Brough to sell or buy a horse should have made every mistake previously so that he was alert to all the dodges! There is a classic tale of a farmer who sold a horse in the morning and, unwittingly, bought back the same horse in the afternoon. In the interim, it had been given a special grooming, and was now actually of a different colour.

For the young people, fair-time is the opportunity to establish or sustain friendships, many of which lead to marriage. It is no wonder that the young folk are looking at their best when they arrive in the Eden Valley in May and September.

Above, left: Travellers on the Maryport-Carlisle road.
Left: Happy wanderers – gypsy children "on the road."
Above: Displaying the prowess of a good shaft horse at Appleby Fair which, held in the spring, attracts a huge crowd of travellers from all over the country. No one can fail to notice a horse that is running, and great showmanship attends this part of a business transaction. The caravans of the visitors used to stretch along the road towards Long Marton, and were lately confined to Gallows Hill.

The Beckoning Hills

THE HILLS of Lakeland were called "fells" by the old Norse settlers; they occupy most of the space, dominating the lakes and narrow dales. For centuries, they were the haunt only of the local people, and especially the farmers with their mountaineering sheep.

From about the time of the Romantic Period, which began towards the end of the 18th century, the fells became appealing to visitors, but it was not until the 19th century that the modern sport of rock-climbing developed (though many of our Lakeland shepherds were no mean cragsmen, developing their techniques through the necessity of having to rescue cragfast sheep).

Our picture (left) shows an enthusiast for mountaineering posing in the safety of a local photographer's studio. He has a hempen rope and ice axe. The climbers of the 19th century were voluble recorders of what they saw and did, as anyone can see who visits a second-hand bookshop in Lakeland. Some of them were fond of gathering at the inn near the head of Wasdale, and they were known to perfect their techniques by negotiating a mantelpiece, or ascending the outside of a barn.

Early tourists were conveyed up some of the fells on ponyback; and now a host of people follow well-worn paths to the tops of the fells. These paths are now so well used that they are visible, in clear conditions, to anyone who is walking on the Pennines!

Radiating like immense spokes from the rocky hub of Lakeland, the fell ranges offer exercise and spiritual uplift to visitors, some of whom — sadly — do not equip themselves for the sudden changes of weather for which the region is famous. The selfless rescue organisations must periodically go into action to rescue people overcome by grim conditions only a mile or so from the relative comfort of a Lakeland dalehead.

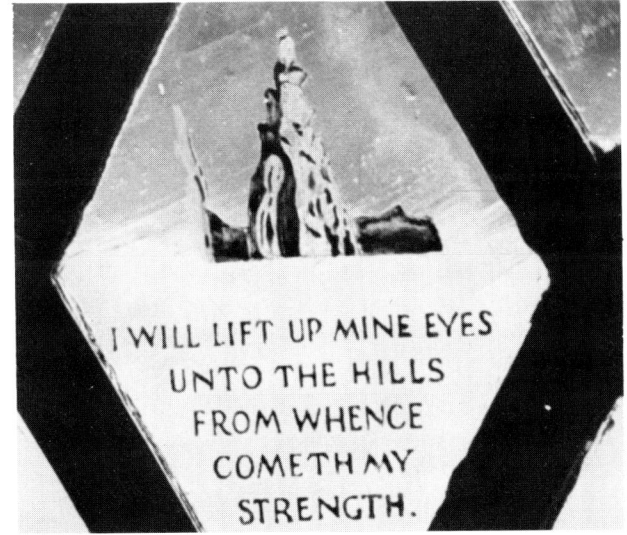

Above: A visitor to the old refreshment hut which stood on Skiddaw. **Above, right**: Taken during Easter, 1904, this study of Bow Fell in snow — with some hardy Edwardian ramblers — was captioned "Farthest South". Winter is slow to relinquish its grip on our Lakeland Fells. **Right**: A quotation scratched in glass on a window in the tiny church at Wasdale Head. In the yard of this church have been buried a number of people who lost their lives during mountaineering jaunts.

The Metal-Workers

SMITHS WERE, indeed, mighty men in a community before communications were improved and our Lakeland farmers and villagers were able to get goods and services from the nearest town; this sounded the death knell for many village crafts. The obvious product of the smithy was a horseshoe, made from wrought-iron. The man at work in our picture above was Jim Kirkby, of Grasmere. Notice the leathern bellows on the left.

The Lakeland blacksmith also hooped the wooded wheels which had been made by the joiner. He made a large number of fastenings and other objects, and a visit to a Lakeland barn reveals the craftsmanship of blacksmiths long dead, for even the nails were once made locally.

One remembers the clear ringing of hammer against anvil and the roar of the open fire; the showers of sparks and the glow from a horseshoe fresh from the fire.

Some of the blacksmith's techniques were demonstrated at an outdoor event at Appleby (the average smithy was notoriously gloomy, inhibiting photography). There was a time when every tradesman had a horse and vehicle. A special winter task was frost-sharpening the shoes of horses so that the animals could keep their feet on slippery roads. The farrier also coped with all manner of foot ailments, and he corrected faults in the horse's gait.

An Element of Fun

IF YOU WENT to have a photograph taken in the old days, the exposure depended greatly on the strength of the daylight; it could last for several seconds. Those were the days of large plate cameras, and the photographic emulsion was slow. In our picture, one of the Abraham family – famous in the photographic history of Lakeland – demonstrates the use of a studio camera.

A consequence was that subjects in a studio kept a fixed expression, and we have an impression that they were dull of spirit. Life in Lakeland has often been a grim struggle for existence, yet the local people kept a sense of fun.

Light-heartedness in Lakeland tends to be reflected by wit – the spontaneous comment – rather than humour, which is contrived. There is also a touch of fantasy, as in the story of the folk of Borrowdale, who built a wall across the valley to retain the cuckoo, preventing it from taking the good weather away with it!

In the picture on the right, E. R. Denwood and R. W. Hall are occupying a coracle they made for a voyage from Cockermouth to Workington. They were not out to prove anything, but simply rejoiced in doing something different which would make others smile. The farmer's sense of fun was often demonstrated in the scarecrows made in arable country. Our print shows that a Teddy Bear was transformed from a snug bedroom to a windy field to discourage rooks, one of which was slain to act as a deterrent to others.

Above: A Lakeland farmer, his facial expression caught in a moment of merriment. It was at the market, or on a summer sports occasion, that a normally solitary and taciturn man could relax and enliven a conversation with sparkling wit. Such a man was good at responding to visitors. One off-comer looked at a local hill and said: "You must have been up there a hundred times." "Nay," the farmer replied, "but dog 'as."

Left: Much effort was put into making this ice-house at Cockermouth in 1895. **Above:** Gurning through a horse-collar, an old Lakeland feat that tested the elasticity of the muscles. **Below:** Visitors in a joyful mood. Morris-dancers at Skelwith Bridge.

HAYMAKING IN LITTLE LANGDALE

WASHING DAY IN NEWLANDS VALE